OUT OF MY LANE

OUT OF MY LANE

LEVELING THE PLAYING FIELD FOR IRAQI WOMEN

Nancy —

Eileen Padberg

EILEEN PADBERG

Printed in the United States of America

Library of Congress Control Number: 2017961204

ISBN Paperback: 978-1-947368-40-8
ISBN eBook: 978-1-947368-41-5

Cover Design: Mitransh Parihar
Interior Design: Ghislain Viau

Contents

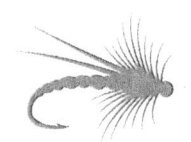

Chapter 1

Iraq Calling: Why I Went

Friday, June 25, 2004. I'm ok and will send a more detailed email later today. Violence is escalating. We are on lockdown; no one leaves the Green Zone for the next two weeks. A mortar hit about 120 yards from the end of our compound a couple of days ago and killed a young Iraqi worker. Our guard rushed over to help him, but he died in his arms. Our building is pretty safe and I feel comfortable with our guards, although I take nothing for granted.

You ou may wonder how a sixty-year-old, card-carrying Republican woman with a thriving political consulting business in Orange County, California, ended up sending out e-mails like the one above from the middle of the Iraq War. I wondered about that myself sometimes—especially when running toward a Black Hawk helicopter in 118-degree temperatures, in a sandstorm, wearing a forty-four-pound flak jacket. But I never wondered for long. I had responsibilities to the women whose futures were in my hands, and to their families. Once I'd boarded that flight to Kuwait from Washington D.C., there was no turning back. I could not dwell on being in the middle of a war.

In the aftermath of the 2003 Iraq invasion, Congress appropriated $18.4 billion in taxes for construction and repair of the country's infrastructure. The purpose of this outlay was to address Iraq's decades of neglect—this was a nation that had been at war or occupied by a foreign power since the seventeenth century. During his dictatorship, Saddam Hussein reportedly built between eighty and two hundred fifty mega-palaces all across Iraq in order to assert his authority, beginning (depending on which accounts one reads) at the end of the Gulf War in 1991. The rumor was that he never stayed at a single one for more than two days—likely for safety and security reasons. His staff never knew where he would go next; consequently, each palace would nightly prepare huge, elaborate dinners for him and his Republican Guard. During the course of his reign, Saddam essentially looted his country, allowing a nation of twenty-seven million people to completely fall apart.

In garnering support for the invasion, President George W. Bush had promised Iraqi women that the United States would restore the rights that had been stripped from them over the course of Saddam's thirty-three-year reign. Iraqi women are tough, motivated, resilient, and clever. On the day we sat in our living rooms watching the towering statue of Saddam being knocked from its pedestal, they were already out organizing to reclaim their rights. Later, however, the United States supported only three of the twenty-five capable, educated women appointed to the 250-member transitional government we'd put in place.

The constitution of 1970 had granted women equal rights, which endured until Saddam came to power in 1979, and even through the early years under his Ba'ath Party. Women could own property, enjoy freedom from workplace harassment (years ahead of America), obtain five years' worth of maternity benefits (again, miles ahead of the United States), wear anything they wanted in public, vote, run for office, and live without restrictions on their mobility and their access to employment. They were encouraged to become educated; in fact there were reportedly more female engineers per capita in Iraq than anywhere else in the Middle East.

However, when Saddam began losing popularity amid a series of failed wars and rising poverty, he expanded his circle to include deeply conservative religious leaders. In 1993 he launched a "Faith Campaign" as a way of reaching out to fundamentalist religious segments of Iraq's population—and women soon found their rights sharply curtailed. His regime brutally oppressed the Shiites and Kurds, among others, but women suffered the most . . . as they do all over the world.

While many of Iraqi women's lost rights were reinstated after the 2003 invasion, only a scant few of the Pentagon's reconstruction contracts included plans to provide Iraqi women (who made up about 65 percent of the population) the opportunity to pursue careers in the two important ministries I was assigned to work with: the Ministry of Water Resources (which was headed by a man who did not think women should get the training that we were offering) and the Ministry of Public Works (which was headed by a woman). Opportunities like these would have enabled them to play a key role in the rebuilding of Iraq, rather than just toiling away at menial jobs. When we brought together the women who worked at the Ministry of Water Resources, they told us that some of them had been in their jobs or assignments for over twenty years without any advanced training. The advanced training opportunities that provided a way to move up went only to the men in the Ministry.

Being a Woman in Orange County

At that time I lived in Orange County, California, where I had built a three-decades-long career in professional consulting and political management, working to empower women and female candidates through the many campaigns I managed and supported. Orange County was defined by its generations-old, deeply homogenized, conservative

Republican, white male syndicate. Breaking through the barriers erected by that syndicate took years, and it's still a task in progress.

Here's an anecdote to give you some idea of the non-inclusive culture that went unchallenged for many years in Orange County: In the late 1980s, my business partner organized a Republicans for Clinton effort in the area. He had several high-powered women involved with this campaign, including a developer and a member of the county board of supervisors. Within three years, the Republican establishment had helped to bankrupt the developer and run her out of town. The woman on the county board of supervisors remained where she was—once you win an election in Orange County (normally an against-all-odds struggle for a woman), you get reelected in perpetuity—but they were always after her, launching defamatory character attacks and otherwise hindering her.

When retired Superior Court Judge Judith Ryan, a candidate of mine, tried to unseat thirteen-year veteran Republican congressman Bob Dornan in the 1992 primary, the Orange County Republican chairman at the time did everything he could to dissuade her from running against a sitting Republican congressman. It was sort of an unwritten law that a Republican (especially a woman) must not challenge a sitting incumbent. In a similar situation, a respected Newport Beach city councilwoman was going to challenge an incumbent Republican male in the primary. She got the same treatment. I was publicly quoted as saying that "these guys believe in free and open elections around the world, but they don't believe in free and open elections in their own county."

On some fronts it's still tough. That is not to say the region where I forged a successful career by building other people's careers wasn't good to me; in most ways it was. It's just that I chose a challenging path: outspoken support of women in the face of Republican Party resistance. There were lots of walls to scale and myths to debunk, which in some ways fortified and motivated me to handle what I would encounter in Iraq.

I was also raised in a blue-collar household where hard work was valued highly—except that women in our family were encouraged to become teachers, nuns, or wives and mothers. My father and grandfather were carpenters, however, so perhaps the proclivity for building is in my DNA. When I was asked to go into a war zone and lay the groundwork for women to help reconstruct Iraq, one might say the family tradition of building things continued.

Really . . . Why Me?

In 2003, a colleague at another firm received a call from a client who was bidding with another global engineering firm in a joint venture to bid on an RFP (request for proposal) to rebuild the water infrastructure in Iraq. The RFP included a requirement that any proposal address the lack of opportunity for women in the country; this requirement consisted of one sentence: "provide a plan to include the Iraqi women in the reconstruction process." It really wasn't my colleague's area of expertise, so she asked me if I would be interested in putting together a plan that she could submit to her client. Over two weeks in November 2003, I drafted a comprehensive plan focusing on the need for women to have a level playing field that afforded them opportunities to build businesses and to obtain jobs that would lead to careers in which they could advance. I have always believed that unless women have a stake in the economy, democracy will fail in any nation. I knew nothing about Iraq at the time, and nothing about the Middle East, but I knew history, and I knew that women's participation was necessary for Iraq's economic success.

Months later, I was notified that the joint venture contract had been won. The women's plan component had received high marks, and the bidder asked me if I would go to Iraq to implement it. I really hate guns and am not an advocate of war, so although I felt strongly that the plan needed to be put to work, I turned them down—adamantly.

Some background: A lot of US government money at the time was going to men through construction contracts, and to NGOs to help low-income women learn such things as how to sew—not exactly a career-building skill. I believed women needed the kind of training that would enable them to move up in government—in the two largest of the ministries that were putting Iraq back together: the Ministry of Water Resources and the Ministry of Municipalities and Public Works.

There was a time in that country when opportunities for women had been better. Iraqi men had gone off to war numerous times in the country's history, and just as in the United States during World War II, many of those men were away for years, and many lost their lives—so the women would temporarily take their jobs. But much like American women in the 1940s, they never got titles or decent salaries, and when the wars were over most returned to being wives and mothers.

I imagined a three-legged stool that Iraqi women were going to need to support their futures:

1. Getting them jobs
2. Helping them to start new businesses by competing for US government contracts
3. Providing training programs to those women who already worked in the government ministries so they could move up and get the titles and salaries they deserved

After I initially turned down the offer to go to Iraq, I was asked to give it some additional thought. I had been doing some downsizing, possibly with an eye to retirement, and I'd moved my office into my home. But on the other hand, I was also opening up some space in my life for new experiences—for example, I was considering learning to surf, although I don't even know how to swim. This seemed like an ambitious task that would get me out of my comfort zone.

As I began to think through the Iraq job, I realized that after thirty years of professional consulting, and political management, and working to empower women, this was the chance of a lifetime. I'd be out there pretty much without a parachute . . . or a surfboard. It was time to walk the walk—both as an American and as a woman.

I'd rush headlong into the unknown. Why not? I was sixty. I'd had the same clients for a number of years. Maybe it was time to do something entirely different—something that would force me to ride a bigger wave than the ones I saw each day along the California coast.

Iraq. From comfort zone to Green Zone. I committed to six months . . . which would ultimately turn into twenty-two.

Iraq would not be my first brush with an emerging democracy. I was a volunteer for an organization in Washington that sent experienced political and government consultants into countries that were experiencing their first democratic elections. In the course of that volunteer effort, I'd been in Guatemala, Sri Lanka, the former Soviet Union,

Kazakhstan, Kyrgyzstan, and Indonesia. But Iraq would be my first experience in a war zone (unless you counted Orange County, California, as a war zone for a moderate Republican woman!).

I framed this as an adventure. It was the opportunity of a lifetime to work with a fledgling democracy, to serve my country, and to test my strength and my commitment to helping women in an environment I knew nothing about. Many of my friends and colleagues were aghast at my decision; when they asked me why I would ever go to a place like that, my response was always, "Why *wouldn't* I go?"

Leaving for Iraq

As steadfast as I now was in my resolve to go, I had enough humility to know I'd need help. I knew nothing about the terrain from a geographical, cultural, or linguistic standpoint. In short I spoke none of the "languages" I'd need. I started looking to recruit an Iraqi-American to go with me. Through the Internet I found Esra, who had been a translator at one of the receptions President Bush gave for Iraqi-American women at the White House. Esra was a savvy twenty-four-year-old bank branch manager near San Diego, so I drove down to meet her and recruit her.

Esra and her family had escaped Iraq in 1990, when she was a child, and spent two years in a refugee camp on the Iraq–Saudi Arabia border. They eventually landed in Irvine,

California, having been granted asylum under the auspices of Catholic Charities. They worked hard and became US citizens.

Esra's parents returned to Iraq in 2003, at the outset of the Iraq War, hoping to reclaim their property. Her father's agenda also included helping to put the country back together now that it was rid of Saddam. Esra missed her parents and wanted to see them again. She was also fluent in Arabic, and she knew the culture. She was a very smart young woman from a well-respected tribe. Her mother was an activist who was well connected in Iraqi political circles and had solid relationships with people at the Ministry of Women, the Ministry of Water Resources, and the Ministry of Municipalities and Public Works.

I needed an assistant and translator, and I knew Esra would be the ideal Iraq War traveling companion—and through it all, as it turned out, she never let me down. I would not have managed the way I did without her and her family: at times they helped us smooth out complications.

They also fed us, which meant a lot in difficult times, when something as simple as a hot meal could lift the spirits. There were some days in the Green Zone when the mortars got so bad the US government couldn't get food into the Green Zone, so it would sit at the airport. We'd be faced with eating MREs—unpalatable government-issued ready-to-eat meals ready to eat—but Esra's mother would bring us roasted chicken, vegetables, french fries, and fresh bread.

On May 26, 2004, Esra and I flew from Los Angeles to Washington and then on to Kuwait. We spent two days in Kuwait, where we were each issued a flak jacket, helmet, and gas mask. (If anything gave me pause, it was definitely the gas mask!)

We proceeded to board a C-130 military transport to Baghdad with three large pieces of luggage each. I had no idea, when we landed at the Baghdad military airport, that the paving was all stones. Imagine trying to roll three large suitcases across stones. Boy, everyone could tell that we were newbies!

Little did I know that C-130, Black Hawk, and Chinook helicopters would become our standard modes of transportation in the war zone. We'd also get to avail ourselves of the occasional Humvee and the "up-armored car"—a standard SUV enhanced with bullet-resistant steel, composite material, and ballistic glass. These vehicles provided protection from assault rifles, carjackings, fire, armor-piercing rounds, and roadside bombs, but were not impervious to blowing up and turning over.

I said a prayer.

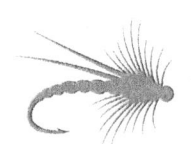

Chapter 2

Acceptable Weight Gain:
40 lb. Flak Jacket, 9 lb. Helmet, Cumbersome Gas Mask—Oh, My!

July 2, 2004. I don't get much news—the mess halls have satellite, but the soldiers are usually watching some sort of sports. I am brave enough to come to Baghdad, but not brave enough to change the channel when 500 guys with guns are watching sports . . . so I occasionally see Fox & British version of CNN at the gym (which I just started going to). There are so many men there that it intimidates me (that's funny). The news is not filtered at all. However, the only newspaper is the Stars and Stripes, and it is very biased. I do go online each day and take a look at the Washington Post and LA Times, but don't of course have time to read all the articles.

The Iraqis here give me their take on what is happening outside the Green Zone (there is lots of Iraqi radio), and it appears that the Iraqis are taking the handover very well, although there are still some problems. There is no question in my mind that the Iraqis want us here—I see it every day. They know that there is no way that they could get rid of Saddam and repair the years of damage and neglect to everything here without us. They want to learn and they want our help. I really do believe that some form of democracy will take hold here, but it won't be easy. People are just not used to making decisions; they were never allowed to.

Entering the Green Zone

The Green Zone, more formally known as the International Zone, is a 3.9-square-mile area of Baghdad. It houses government-occupied buildings and is bordered by massive concrete barriers on the north and west sides and by the Tigris River to the south and east. For the duration of my stay and for some years after, there were numerous security checkpoints regulating traffic into the area. Vehicles were checked for bombs and Iraqis on foot were patted down. This was to be my life in Iraq.

About ten thousand Iraqi squatters moved into the Green Zone when war broke out. Most Iraqis had never seen the government section (the Green Zone), so they swarmed the area and stole everything that they could get their hands on. It would have made for bad press to push them out of the Green Zone, so we just had to try to live with the risk and inconvenience they represented. Security routinely peppered us with admonitions about situational awareness: there was a $300,000 price on the heads of all American women.

"You don't know who's around," we'd be warned.

"Don't walk anywhere alone."

"Don't pick up anything from the street." Even a one hundred dollar bill could be rigged to detonate.

"Don't take any cabs."

"You can't take food from anybody."

There were several eating establishments in the Green Zone that we were told by our security not to patronize, but sometimes we did anyway. Five months after I arrived, in October 2004, Al Qaeda-related suicide bombings would destroy two favorites: the Bazaar, which sold everything from shoes to hand lotion to Iraqi knickknacks, and the Green Zone Café, one of our favorite places to eat.

On January 1, 2009, the Green Zone would be handed over to Iraqi security forces, and on October 4, 2015, it would open to the public . . . with restrictions. But when I was there, internal perils notwithstanding, it was considered a bubble of security (hence its nickname, The Bubble) for the US military, US contractors, the Army Corps of Engineers, US embassy personnel, and any wildcard citizens (*ahem*) who had been sent to see if they could effect change. I understood that I was coming to Iraq under the auspices of the contractor that had won the bid, but all too soon Esra and I would find ourselves basically on our own. (More on that later.)

If we wanted to venture out of the Green Zone, we needed approval and acres of security around us. However, I have to confess: Experiencing cabin fever and needing a break from our ten-hours-a-day, seven-days-a-week job (minus Friday mornings, which were a religious time for Iraqis), Esra and I did head out a time or two with her mother—without availing ourselves of security protocols beforehand. But we understood the consequences. If we were harmed or killed outside the Green Zone with no security, without having obtained prior approval, there would be no life insurance payments for our loved ones. On those rare occasions, curiosity and desire trumped reason.

When we first landed in Baghdad, we were met by a steel-plated bus known as the Rhino, which had minuscule windows (over which curtains were drawn) and a bank vault–style door. It was like riding in a tomb, which I hoped did not portend anything for us. We were traveling through the Red Zone (a military term for any area outside the ten square kilometers of the Green Zone—essentially, most of

Baghdad), and it was imperative that any Americans on the bus be concealed. I could hear mortars, and I had a visceral reaction; I *felt* for the first time that I was smack in the middle of a war. I felt it in my bones.

Once we had arrived safely at our destination, and before we got to our living quarters, we were whisked to the mess hall, or DFAC. It was about 7:00 p.m., and we had to eat immediately, because after the DFAC closed, you couldn't eat until the next morning; there were strict times set for when it opened and closed. It would be a while before I got friends to send care packages with items like coffee and creamer, cookies, and wine—which had to be labeled "shampoo" or "grape juice." I even got cigars sent from my best friend Alix in Florida, who owned a catalogue cigar company; those made me quite popular! I handed them out to the troops when we traveled, or for their Thursday night breaks. Alix became a sort of quartermaster, able to get and ship anything that Esra and I needed: makeup, lotion, shoes, socks, Sweet'N Low, books, and even my fishing gear!

There were no seating arrangements in the mess hall; rather, it was a noisy throng of generals, enlisted men (including our guards), contractors, engineers, embassy staff, Iraqi staff, and others. An ominous black weapon lay beside each soldier, within easy reach, though cartridges were emptied at the door. We had to step over the weapons to get to a seat. It was an out-of-body experience for me—especially in the beginning. I definitely wasn't "in Kansas" anymore. No water glasses were being refilled or crumbs deftly swept away while we ordered flourless chocolate cake with raspberry coulis. Meat was flown in frozen, and they would boil it to make hamburgers. The smell was awful, and it would sometimes hit us first thing in the morning.

Our quarters were in a former high school built for the children of Saddam's Republican Guard. Each classroom contained five or six beds—no dressers, and no partitions. Nothing at all between the beds for privacy. My first reaction was, "God—this is where I'm going to live?" Just fifteen days earlier, I had been living in a 3,100-square-foot home in Laguna Niguel, California.

Esra and I roomed with a female engineer from South Africa and an Iraqi-American woman from Michigan whose surroundings made her cry for the first couple of weeks because she was "going to have to live like this." In the beginning I came close to crying myself, never having so much as lived in a college dorm, much less a cramped environment like this one.

Mortars were our 6:30 a.m. wake-up call. You could literally set your alarm clock by the one that was lobbed at that time. We'd go from under the sheets to under the bed—grabbing helmets and flak jackets on the way. Explosions went off around us 24–7—and the helicopters flying overhead were likewise nonstop. You almost got used to it, just as you might become accustomed to a persistent subway rattle or your neighbor's pesky power mower or California earthquakes; familiar ambient sounds become a part of the background over time.

Bombs and Bureaucracies

One of the first things we learned in Baghdad was how to check for car bombs (on the few occasions we were lucky enough to corral a car). We learned how to scrupulously check under the car, under the hood, and above the wheels. Those and other security protocols we adhered to were daunting at first, and they only served to reinforce the unsettling knowledge that I'd put Esra's life in jeopardy by bringing her with me to Iraq. It had been her decision, of course, but I felt wholly responsible for her. What kept us going was our commitment to helping thousands of oppressed, educated women change their lives—to helping them reclaim the work to which they were entitled, thereby potentially altering the course of the country's history as well.

Our conditions may have been challenging, but Iraqis' living conditions were more so. In addition to constant threats of kidnapping and death, they lived in poverty—in circumstances that included a mere two to three hours a day of electricity, despite 120-degree temperatures during many months of the year and biting cold in winter. There was no air conditioning, no heat, and questionable sanitary conditions. Saddam had ensured all of that.

For the first four months we were in Iraq, we did have air conditioning and heat in our living and working quarters—but we had nothing in the way of equipment or other support to do our jobs. We had no phones and no computers. The only way to check and send e-mail, or to use the Internet for research for the programs we were there to institute, was to briefly purloin someone else's computer who might have gone to lunch or dinner or left for the day.

Esra and I were last on the list for everything. It seemed no one felt our program was a priority. Their priorities were to get architects and engineers in and buildings built. Period. Even the two engineering firms that had sent us to Iraq had not briefed their own employees that they were sending over two women for a specific purpose. If not for our own initiative—if we'd elected to sit there and wait for any of this to change—we'd have been sipping coffee and staring out the window for months, which is not uncommon in a bureaucracy.

Living, Working, and Fishing

At this point I want to make clear that the purpose of this chapter is not to pour out a cascade of complaints. Rather, it is to illustrate the conditions under which we lived and worked, and to demonstrate how determined we were to advocate for women in Iraq.

Every day it was the same routine. It was Iraqi *Groundhog Day*, and I'd be glancing around for Bill Murray. We awoke to mortar and gunfire and padded down an external walkway to get anywhere in the high school that was our home. If you had to use the women's facilities at night, it was the same thing (I had to prevail upon my friend Julie in California to send me pajamas suitable for public viewing). There was little privacy. In the mornings we wrestled with a cold shower that barely dribbled water.

The DFAC was about half a mile away, and if it was stormy, we plodded through the rain in ankle-deep mud. From there it was about a mile hike to our office, where we started work at 8:00 a.m. The office was in a building that had housed a museum on the main floor, and it was rumored that Saddam had tortured his enemies in the basement. I never went down there myself, as I'm somewhat claustrophobic, but others reported to me that there were indeed chains hanging from a basement wall.

With no technology, we filled dozens of notebooks with ideas to implement programs based on the plan I'd written back in California. Again, though there'd been a mechanism in place to get us to Baghdad, there was no support when we got there. There wasn't even a budget or any kind of funding allocated. We marshaled forces and resources and often used our own funds—for everything from seminars to lunch and snacks, and eventually we were reimbursed. It was all up to us.

We tried to connect with Iraqi businesswomen and organizations in those first few months by venturing over to the US embassy, which was housed in the Republican Palace (in 2009 the embassy would relocate to its own newly constructed, $750-million building). Built by American modernist architect J. Brian Cooper in the 1950s for King Faisal II, the palace was later enlarged by Saddam and had been his venue of choice for entertaining visiting heads of state. In 2003, it became the headquarters of the American occupation and also the primary base of operations for the American diplomatic mission in Iraq until the new embassy opened.

For Esra and me, except for our occasional forays outside the Green Zone to lead seminars and training sessions, the palace was now where we spent much of our time—rallying people to our cause and holding various meetings. It also had a pretty good DFAC, and once we figured that out, we'd schedule meetings in order to have lunch there. On a large or small scale, it's interesting what becomes important when so much of what you're used to taking for granted is not available to you.

The view from the building where our office was located was always filled with things to write home about. Located as we were between the palace and the Red Zone, directly across from a hospital that had been taken over by the US, we'd see fifteen or twenty lumbering tanks roll in each day with soldiers presumably on break. They'd be smoking or eating—laughing, even—just hanging out and grasping at a few minutes of normality amid the omnipresent threat of sudden death.

Interestingly, one of the many obstacles we would repeatedly face was being told both by the Americans we worked with and by the Iraqis that we were "out of our lane," meaning that because we were part of the water reconstruction team, we supposedly were only allowed to deal with the employees of the water ministries and only allowed to train those women who were responding to an RFP affecting the water sector. But it was difficult to ignore that Iraq needed transformation in other walks of life as well, and our objectives always overlapped. It was hard to decide only to help women in these two ministries. Out of my lane or not, my goal was to include as many women as possible in my outreach.

In detail, the program was to focus on creating equal opportunities for women—jobs and career development training programs. We also hoped to build and expand women's small businesses by teaching them how to bid on and win some of the many contracts being awarded through the reconstruction effort, and by providing any technical training needed to execute those contracts. The career development training seminars we were there to implement ranged from gender mainstreaming to budget and finance to computer skills. There would also be a need to teach public speaking: Iraqi women were very quiet when it came to

American men. All the contracts came from the Army Corps of Engineers—and 98 percent of its members were men. We found that women going in for interviews there had been very quiet, so we instituted some public speaking programs, emphasizing the importance of projecting confidence.

In the beginning, I'd determined that the first order of business was to create a job bank so that any and all opportunities could be centralized. In time we'd compiled a list of Iraqi women who were seeking jobs. We would try to hook them up with contractors we met along the way. In addition—and we'll explore this in greater depth later in the book—we developed a list of approximately 350 women-owned businesses capable of bidding on US government contracts. The list was distributed every other month to anyone in Iraq who had the authority to award contracts. This was definitely "out of our lane" . . . and Esra and I couldn't have been more proud of it!

As for our living quarters, following about six or seven months in a converted classroom, we were all moved into the trailers behind the palace. I use the word *trailers* loosely here; they were actually shipping containers that had been "adapted" for human habitation. When the helicopters took off in the morning, the trailers shook. There were other trailers around us in our development, which was officially called Riverside Estates, but affectionately known as Mortar Alley. Sandbags were piled high in front and in back of each trailer to keep shrapnel from going through, should a mortar hit. And yet the roofs of these trailers were so thin I feared even a small rock would puncture them.

Though they registered a notch higher on the privacy meter, these trailers were nowhere near as safe as our school had been. Each "trailer" slept two people, and normally two trailers shared a very small bathroom that held the two together. So instead of five or six people sharing a single classroom with beds and no bathroom, now there were four of us with one very small bathroom.

Our final dwelling would be an ad hoc motel with separate (yes!) nine-by-twelve-foot rooms, each for one person, each with its own bathroom and shower. There was a community room on each floor with a microwave. The average size of a prison cell is nine feet by twelve feet in California—we thought about things like that to lighten the mood. Memories of the large home half a mile from the Pacific Ocean that I'd left behind were fading, sometimes seeming to me like another lifetime, or someone else's life. We finally had our coveted and long anticipated privacy, but it took some getting used to after a yearlong pajama party.

Friday morning and early afternoon until about 2:00 p.m. was our only time off in a seven-day workweek. It was a time of religious observance for the Iraqis, and I soon found my way to the Tigris River. An avid fly fisher, I'd spent time plying my craft in the wilds of Utah, Wyoming, Montana,

Idaho, Belize, Chile, Argentina, and other scenic locales—all infinitely less polluted than the Tigris. Though the carp were plentiful, I was mindful of the badly polluted water, so I tossed them back into the river after catching them.

When I first learned I could fish there, I had a friend send over my fly rod, flies, and anything else I needed. Oddly enough, there were always three or four of us fishing together. I taught some men from the Army Corps of Engineers and soldiers to fly fish and even had some inexpensive rods sent over for them. Fridays were the day we had to clean our living quarters, but fly fishing in the Tigris became a kind of meditation, allowing me to clear my head and regroup, so I always went there first. Then I'd return to clean my room. The desert dust that accumulated throughout the week was awful.

Because we had those mornings off, we went in to work on Fridays until 9:00 or 10:00 p.m., as our contract called for ten- to twelve-hour days. But no matter how late we worked, Fridays were great days. In fact, they were the only days that didn't quite fit the *Groundhog Day* mold.

Chapter 3

Iraqi Women: A Brief Primer

November 13, 2004. Two nights ago, a mortar hit our trailer park. I was helping my roommate pack for her R&R. It was about 8:00 p.m., and it was so close we could hear the whiz. We both hit the floor, reaching for our vests and helmets. It was the closest I have come. The night before, a mortar hit the trailer park right next to us and killed three people. Three of our Iraqi guards (on the gate into our office building) were kidnapped last week; they found their bodies the day before yesterday. My friend Claudia emailed me this morning: "Come home and make your biggest risk the 405 freeway like the rest of us."

I went to Iraq to help that country's capable, motivated, educated women obtain what they'd worked so hard for—what their male counterparts had, and what had been taken from them in 1993 by Saddam Hussein's Ba'ath regime. I wanted them to have what they were entitled to by virtue of their credentials.

But first, just who are these women?

Women make up 62 to 65 percent of Iraqi society. The 1980–1988 Iran-Iraq War killed a large number of Iraq's male population, leaving legions of widows and other single women to fend for themselves. Single status was and still is a black mark that subjects women to harsh social treatment, including ostracism.

Without their men, these women needed to work. And the social implications of being widowed or single aside, they deserved and *wanted* to work—as they always had.

Women had more rights in Iraq than anywhere else in the Middle East, except Israel, until after the Gulf War. In the distant past, Iraqi women had always had their own businesses. This norm may have reflected the life of the Prophet Muhammad's first wife, Khadija, who was a wealthy, self-made merchant when he married her. But after Iraq's defeat in the Gulf War in 1991 and the Faith Campaign that soon followed, women's businesses, the positions they held, and their overall status began to deteriorate. Women's rights were taken from them, and they were systematically pushed out of the workforce.

Until the 1990s, women were considered integral to the political and economic development of Iraq. Prior to the

Ba'ath Party's coup d'état in 1968, a robust civil society had existed, including a fair number of women's organizations dedicated to the promotion and protection of women. The Ba'ath Party dismantled most of these groups after it seized power, establishing in their place the General Federation of Iraqi Women. The GFIW successfully implemented state policy, reportedly by running more than 250 urban and rural community centers offering job training, social, and educational programs for women. It also acted as a conduit for state propaganda, however, and Iraqi women claim that as a political arm of the party, the GFIW was destructive to women's issues and did not "reflect or represent the struggle of millions of oppressed Iraqi women."[1] Fundamentally, Saddam's adoption of Islamic and tribal traditions as a political tool in order to consolidate power had a grave effect on women.

There are still many women-owned businesses in the country, however. Much as we do here, women would bid on construction contracts that might include laying pipes—a job for which they would hire men to work under their supervision. Most educated Iraqi women speak very good or at least passable English. They are also dignified and proud, as I discovered when I was there, and for that reason they

---

1 Human Rights Watch Briefing Paper, "Background on Women's Status in Iraq Prior to the Fall of the Saddam Hussein Government: November, 2003," https://www.hrw.org/legacy/backgrounder/wrd/iraq-women.htm.

may not step up and ask a foreigner—particularly a male foreigner—to repeat something said to them of which they are uncertain. Esra and I learned that it was sometimes necessary to ask them if they understood what had been said in order to make sure they were clear about it. We also had to teach them to speak up during meetings with male hiring managers when vying for contracts.

After the United Nations Security Council imposed sanctions on Iraq after its invasion of Kuwait in 1990, Iraqis had virtually no interaction with Americans—and therefore little or no opportunity to practice their English skills, which were important during the US reconstruction efforts.

When having lunch or business meetings with Iraqi women, I found that their everyday complaints were the same as ours—men, children, and being in the working world. It made me realize that women all over the globe are the same, and in a strange way, it brought me some comfort about being in a war zone.

In my twenty-two months in Iraq, I found that many Iraqi women had a wonderful sense of humor. They are also indescribably brave. The hardships and tragedies they faced on a daily basis were unrelenting—including not knowing, when they sent their children off to school, if they'd ever see them alive again. A sense of humor makes the difference between sanity and emotional collapse.

Divorce rates in Iraq are reportedly on the rise. Obtaining a divorce, however, leaves women vulnerable to social rejection because they are unmarried, and subjects them to forced isolation or sexual abuse within the confines of secret marriages.[2] When a woman is on her own, her husband's family must take care of her, which presents problems of its own.

Iraqi women are educated. This tradition goes back decades; for much of his reign, Saddam wanted women in Iraq to be educated because it made him look good in the eyes of the rest of the world. Even today, there are more female engineers in Iraq than anywhere else in the Middle East. Seventy percent of Iraq's agricultural workforce is also made up of women.

In the 1960s and '70s, women were free to dress as they chose; it was not uncommon to see miniskirts in the nightclubs—something Esra's mother experienced firsthand. In 1970, the New Interim Constitution for the Republic of Iraq, also known as the Iraqi Provisional Constitution, provided for equal rights for women, including the right to attend school. At that time, schools became public and free at all levels (although this is no longer the case). The constitution also allowed women to vote and run for office (since 1980, at least), and to drive and to own property,

---

2 Ali Abel Sadah, "Iraq Divorce Rates, Social Problems on Rise," *Al-Monitor* (January 17, 2013), http://www.al-monitor.com/pulse/originals/2013/01/iraq-divorce-increase-violence.html.

and as I mentioned earlier, it offered them protection from workplace harassment.

After the United States deposed Saddam in 2003, the Bush administration's promise to restore women's rights and rebuild their country made Iraqi women confident enough to demand 40 percent representation in their government. After marching, holding rallies, and arguing the matter for two years, however, they ended up with 25 percent—the minimum mandated by the country's constitution. Many women claim that even with one-quarter representation, they still have no power.

Interestingly, whether they have the power they need or not, Iraq still outranks the United States in the representation of women in government in the developed world—American women make up only 19 percent of our government. In fact the United States is number 97 on a list of 187 countries in terms of the representation of women in their parliaments or legislatures, ranking just above Kazakhstan, which is number 98 on the list. Rwanda's women are better represented in government at 39 percent; South Africa and Cuba each have 36 percent female representation, and even Afghanistan has 27 percent. So the United States has a distance to go—but I digress.

Once it became known what Esra and I were trying to do, we found that women were so determined to avail themselves of these opportunities that they risked beatings, rape, and